Navigating the Cyber Battlefield: A Comprehensive Guide for Business Leaders

In the ever-evolving realm of cybersecurity, business leaders face a relentless challenge: safeguarding their organizations from a myriad of sophisticated cyber threats. The stakes have never been higher, as compromised data can lead to irreparable financial losses, reputational damage, and even legal repercussions.

This book, "Welcome to the Cyber Battlefield," serves as a comprehensive guide for business leaders, equipping them with the knowledge and strategies necessary to navigate the ever-shifting cybersecurity landscape. Through a blend of insightful analysis and practical guidance, the book empowers leaders to understand the evolving nature of cyber threats, recognize the critical importance of cybersecurity, and implement effective measures to protect their organizations.

Stats:

- The global cost of cybercrime is estimated to reach $10.5 trillion annually by 2025 (Cybersecurity Ventures).

- Ransomware attacks grew by 41% in 2022, with the average ransom payment reaching $1.8 million (Check Point).

- Phishing attacks increased by 48% in the first half of 2022, with reports of 11,395 incidents costing businesses a total of $12.3 million (Security Intelligence).

- In 2022, 71% of businesses reported falling victim to ransomware attacks (Unitrends).

- The average cost of a data breach in the United States in 2022 was $9.44 million (IBM).

Examples:

- In 2021, Colonial Pipeline, a major U.S. fuel pipeline operator, was forced to shut down its operations after a ransomware attack. The company reportedly paid $4.4 million in ransom to the attackers.

- In 2017, Equifax, a major credit reporting agency, suffered a data breach that exposed the personal information of over 147 million people. The company settled with the Federal Trade Commission (FTC) for $700 million.

- In 2016, Yahoo disclosed a data breach that affected over 3 billion users. The company's stock price fell by over 30% following the disclosure of the breach.

Anecdotes:

1. **A Costly Phishing Incident:**

   - Real-world consequences of a phishing attack witnessed.

   - Highlights the severe financial and reputational impact on an organization.

   As an IT leader, I've witnessed firsthand the devastating impact of phishing attacks on organizations. In one particularly memorable case, an employee received a seemingly innocuous email that appeared to be from a trusted vendor. The email contained a link that prompted the employee to enter their login credentials.

   Unfortunately, the link led to a cleverly crafted phishing website that mirrored the design of the vendor's portal. The employee, unaware of the deception, entered their credentials, unknowingly handing over their access to the vendor's network.

   The consequences of this phishing attack were severe. The attackers gained access to sensitive customer data and financial information. The organization faced significant financial losses, reputational damage, and legal repercussions.

   This incident highlighted the importance of robust cybersecurity training and awareness programs. Employees must be equipped with the knowledge and skills to identify and avoid phishing scams. Regular security assessments and incident response plans are also crucial for mitigating the risks of these attacks.

2. **A Password Security Wake-Up Call:**

   - A personal experience with weak passwords and a compromised account.

   - The transformation in password management practices and advocating for stronger policies.

In the past, I've admitted to using easily guessable passwords for both personal and professional accounts. I justified this habit by claiming it was a matter of convenience. However, I eventually came to realize that this practice was a major security risk.

My wake-up call came when I received a notification from my personal email provider alerting me to suspicious login attempts. Upon further investigation, I discovered that my account had been compromised due to a weak password.

This incident prompted me to make a significant change in my password habits. I started using strong, unique passwords for all my accounts and enabled two-factor authentication whenever possible. I also advocated for stricter password policies within our organization to ensure that everyone was taking cybersecurity seriously.

This experience taught me that password security is not a matter of convenience; it's a critical component of overall cybersecurity posture. Organizations must prioritize password management practices to protect their data and assets from unauthorized access.

Allow me to introduce myself. With a comprehensive understanding of the ever-evolving cyber threat landscape, my journey in the IT industry spans three decades, encompassing roles in data management, systems analysis, DevOps, security, cloud operations, data center operations, and architectural design. I've been on the front lines, witnessing the rise of sophisticated cyber threats and, more importantly, crafting and implementing strategies that shield organizations from the devastating impacts of cyberattacks.

My expertise doesn't stop at technical know-how—it extends to a deep understanding of business processes and risk management principles. I'm here not just to share information but to empower you with actionable strategies tailored to your organization's unique needs and objectives.

The ethos underlying this book is one of preparedness, awareness, and proactive defense. It emphasizes the need for business leaders to embrace cybersecurity as a critical component of their overall business strategy, rather than an afterthought or an IT-only concern.

The book's perspective is rooted in the belief that cybersecurity is a shared responsibility, requiring collaboration and vigilance from all organizational levels. It emphasizes the importance of fostering a cybersecurity culture within organizations, where every employee plays a role in identifying, preventing, and responding to cyber threats.

In essence, "Welcome to the Cyber Battlefield" is a call to arms for business leaders, empowering them to take charge of their organizations' cybersecurity posture and safeguard their valuable assets in the face of relentless cyber threats. By embracing the ethos of preparedness, awareness, and proactive defense, business leaders can navigate the cyber battlefield with confidence and resilience.

Understanding the Cyber Threat Landscape

In today's interconnected world, businesses face a complex and ever-changing array of cybersecurity threats. This chapter, "Decoding the Digital Risks," serves as your essential guide to navigating the intricate web of cyber threats. We will delve deep into the heart of the cyber threat landscape, providing business leaders with the knowledge necessary to fortify their defenses.

Overview of Prevalent Cyber Threats

- Unraveling the Intricacies of Common Cyber Threats:

Cyber threats lurk in the digital shadows, seeking to exploit vulnerabilities and compromise businesses. Let's explore some of the most prevalent cyber threats that businesses face today:

- Malware: Malicious software designed to harm your computer system or network.

- Ransomware: A type of malware that encrypts your files and demands a ransom payment in exchange for the decryption key.

- Phishing: A deceptive technique used to trick users into revealing sensitive information, such as login credentials or credit card details.

- Understanding the Evolution of Cyber Threats and Their Growing Sophistication:

Cybercriminals are constantly evolving their tactics, adapting to new technologies and exploiting emerging vulnerabilities. As businesses become more reliant on digital systems, cyber threats become more sophisticated and damaging.

Case Studies of Real-World Cyberattacks

Analyzing real-world examples can provide valuable insights into the diverse tactics employed by cybercriminals and the consequences of cyberattacks. Let's examine two notable cases:

- WannaCry Ransomware Attack (2017):

The WannaCry ransomware attack, utilizing a leaked NSA exploit, swept across the globe in 2017, crippling organizations and causing billions in damages. This attack highlighted the global reach of cyber threats and the potential for widespread disruption.

- NotPetya (2017):

The NotPetya malware attack, also known as "Cyber Armageddon," caused widespread damage in 2017, targeting multinational corporations and causing billions in losses. This attack demonstrated the destructive potential of cyberattacks and the importance of cyber resilience.

Understanding the Motivations Behind Cybercrime

Cybercriminals are driven by a variety of motives, ranging from financial gain to political agendas. Understanding these motivations can help businesses anticipate and mitigate cyber threats.

- Financial Gain: Many cyberattacks are motivated by financial gain, with cybercriminals seeking to steal sensitive data, such as credit card numbers or customer information, to sell or use for fraudulent activities.

- Political Motives: Cyberattacks can also be motivated by political goals, such as disrupting critical infrastructure, spreading misinformation, or influencing elections.

- State-Sponsored Attacks: In some cases, cyberattacks are carried out by nation-states for espionage, sabotage, or military objectives.

The Economic Impact of Cybersecurity Breaches

Cybersecurity breaches can have far-reaching consequences, causing significant financial losses, damaging reputations, and exposing organizations to legal repercussions.

- Financial Toll: Cybersecurity breaches can result in direct financial losses due to stolen funds, ransom payments, data recovery costs, and operational disruptions.

- Reputation Damage: A cybersecurity breach can severely damage a company's reputation, leading to lost customers, investor distrust, and negative media coverage.

- Legal Ramifications: Organizations can face legal and regulatory consequences for failing to protect sensitive data or complying with cybersecurity laws.

Examples

To illustrate the impact of cyber threats, let's examine some specific examples:

- The Equifax Data Breach (2017):

The Equifax data breach, exposing the personal information of over 147 million people, resulted in a $700 million settlement with the Federal Trade Commission (FTC).

- The Colonial Pipeline Ransomware Attack (2021):

The Colonial Pipeline ransomware attack forced the shutdown of a major U.S. fuel pipeline, leading to disruptions in fuel supply and significant economic losses.

Key Takeaways

As business leaders, it is crucial to develop a nuanced understanding of the cyber threat landscape and take proactive measures to protect your organization. Here are some key takeaways from this chapter:

- Become an Informed Guardian: Develop a comprehensive understanding of the evolving cyber threat landscape and the diverse tactics used by cybercriminals.

- Learn from Real-World Examples: Analyze case studies of real-world cyberattacks to enhance threat awareness and learn from the successes and failures of other organizations.

- Appreciate the Diversity of Motives: Recognize the varied motivations behind cyberattacks, ranging from financial gain to political agendas, and anticipate threats accordingly.

- Grasp the Economic Implications: Understand the profound economic impact of cybersecurity breaches, including financial losses, reputational damage, and legal ramifications.

The Pillars of Cybersecurity

Considering the constantly shifting realm of cybersecurity, erecting a sturdy defense is not merely an option; it's an imperative. In this chapter, we delve into the fundamental pillars that form the bedrock of a resilient cybersecurity strategy. Welcome to "The Pillars of Cybersecurity," where we embark on a journey to fortify your organization against the relentless onslaught of cyber threats.

1. Vulnerability Management Strategies:

In the dynamic world of cybersecurity, vulnerabilities are like cracks in a fortress – they represent weak points that adversaries can exploit to gain unauthorized access. To combat this, vulnerability management strategies are crucial in identifying, prioritizing, and remediating these weaknesses before they can be breached.

Understanding the lifecycle of vulnerabilities is the cornerstone of effective vulnerability management. This involves tracking the emergence, exploitation, and eventual patching of vulnerabilities to ensure timely mitigation.

Implementing proactive vulnerability scanning is akin to having a vigilant sentinel guarding your organization's digital perimeter. Regular scans detect and identify vulnerabilities in your systems and applications before they can be exploited by attackers.

Prioritizing and categorizing vulnerabilities based on risk is essential for allocating resources effectively. By assessing the likelihood of exploitation and the potential impact of a breach, organizations can focus their efforts on the most critical vulnerabilities first.

Establishing a systematic and timely patch management process is like closing the gaps in your digital fortress. This involves promptly applying patches and updates to software and systems, effectively sealing the vulnerabilities identified through the scanning process.

2. Access Control Best Practices:

In the digital realm, access control acts as a gatekeeper, determining who can access sensitive information and resources. By implementing robust access control measures, organizations can prevent unauthorized individuals from gaining access to critical data and systems.

Role-based access control (RBAC) is like assigning specific roles and permissions to each user, ensuring that they have access only to the resources they need to perform their duties. This principle of least privilege minimizes the potential damage that can be caused by a compromised account.

Continuous monitoring and auditing of user access are akin to keeping a watchful eye on the digital gates. Regularly reviewing and analyzing user access patterns can detect anomalies and identify potential breaches before they escalate.

Two-factor authentication (2FA) adds an extra layer of security, acting as a second checkpoint for user verification. By requiring a combination of factors, such as passwords and one-time codes, 2FA significantly reduces the risk of unauthorized access.

3. Data Security Measures and Encryption:

Data is the lifeblood of any organization, and protecting it is paramount. Data security measures are like safeguarding precious assets, ensuring that they remain confidential, integral, and available.

Classifying and categorizing sensitive data are like organizing a treasure trove. Identifying and classifying data based on its sensitivity allows organizations to prioritize protection efforts and implement appropriate security controls.

Encryption techniques for data in transit and at rest are like cloaking data in an impenetrable shield. Encrypting data while it is being transmitted and when it is stored prevents unauthorized access and theft.

Implementing data loss prevention (DLP) measures is akin to erecting a fence around the data vault. DLP solutions monitor and control the movement of sensitive data, preventing unauthorized exfiltration or accidental disclosure.

Securing data in cloud environments is like fortifying an off-site storage facility. Organizations must ensure that their cloud providers implement robust security measures to protect data stored in the cloud.

4. Developing an Incident Response Plan:

Cybersecurity breaches are not a matter of if, but when. An incident response plan is like having a well-rehearsed emergency response team in place, ensuring that the organization can effectively prepare for, respond to, and recover from cyberattacks.

Understanding the critical components of an incident response plan is like knowing the layout of your organization's digital infrastructure. This plan should clearly outline roles, responsibilities, communication protocols, and recovery procedures.

Creating an incident response team and defining roles are like assembling a specialized task force. This team should include experts from IT, security, legal, and communications departments, each with clearly defined roles and responsibilities.

Establishing communication protocols during an incident is like ensuring clear and coordinated communication during a crisis. This involves defining communication channels, establishing notification procedures, and identifying key stakeholders.

Conducting regular drills and simulations to test the effectiveness of the plan are like running regular fire drills. These exercises help identify gaps, refine procedures, and ensure that the team is prepared to respond effectively to real-world incidents.

5. Integrating Cybersecurity into the Organizational Culture:

Cybersecurity is not just about technology; it's about people and their behavior. Integrating cybersecurity into the organizational culture is like weaving it into the fabric of the organization, ensuring that everyone plays a role in protecting the organization's digital assets.

The role of leadership in fostering a cybersecurity culture is like setting the tone for security awareness. Leaders must actively promote cybersecurity.

Creating a Cyber-Aware Workforce

In the relentless battle against cyber threats, your employees are your most crucial asset, forming the human firewall that safeguards your organization's digital assets. Their actions and decisions can either strengthen or weaken your cybersecurity posture. This chapter delves into the critical aspects of empowering your workforce to be vigilant guardians of your digital assets, transforming them from passive bystanders into active participants in cybersecurity defense.

- Cybersecurity Training for Employees: Equipping Your Workforce with Knowledge and Skills

Comprehensive training programs tailored to different roles and responsibilities are essential to equip your employees with the knowledge and skills necessary to navigate the ever-evolving cybersecurity landscape. This includes:

- Understanding the Basics: Provide employees with a foundational understanding of cybersecurity concepts, including common threats, attack methods, and security best practices.

- Real-World Scenarios: Incorporate realistic scenarios and simulations into training programs to enhance practical understanding and decision-making abilities.

- Continuous Learning: Cybersecurity is a dynamic field, and continuous learning is crucial to keep pace with evolving threats and emerging technologies. Establish regular training programs and provide access to up-to-date resources.

- Phishing Awareness and Prevention: Recognizing and Defending Against Deceptive Attacks

Phishing attacks are a common and sophisticated form of cybercrime, often targeting unsuspecting employees. To counter this threat, it is essential to:

- Anatomy of Phishing: Educate employees on the anatomy of phishing attacks, including the tactics employed by cybercriminals, such as social engineering and email spoofing.

- Simulated Phishing Exercises: Implement simulated phishing exercises to provide hands-on experience in identifying and reporting phishing attempts.

- Empowerment and Reporting: Equip employees with tools to effectively identify and report phishing attempts, encouraging them to take ownership of their digital security.

- Best Practices for Password Hygiene: Implementing Strong Password Policies

Passwords are the first line of defense for most digital accounts, making strong password practices essential. This includes:

- Password Strength: Emphasize the importance of using strong, unique passwords, avoiding easily guessable combinations like birthdays or pet names.

- Regular Updates: Implement password policies that mandate regular password updates, preventing the use of compromised credentials for extended periods.

- Two-Factor Authentication: Encourage the adoption of two-factor authentication, adding an extra layer of security beyond passwords.

- Fostering a Culture of Cybersecurity Vigilance: A Shared Responsibility

Cybersecurity is not solely the responsibility of the IT department; it is a shared responsibility that extends across the entire organization. To foster this culture, it is crucial to:

- Shared Responsibility Mindset: Cultivate a shared responsibility mindset among employees, emphasizing that everyone plays a role in protecting digital assets.

- Proactive Reporting: Encourage a proactive approach to reporting security concerns, creating an environment where employees feel comfortable raising potential issues without fear of reprisal.

- Recognition and Celebration: Recognize and celebrate cybersecurity achievements within the organization, reinforcing positive behavior and creating a culture of appreciation for cybersecurity efforts.

- Engaging Employees in the Protection of Digital Assets: A Collaborative Effort

Engaging employees in the protection of digital assets is essential for building a resilient cybersecurity posture. This includes:

- Policy Development and Review: Involve employees in the development and review of cybersecurity policies, fostering a sense of ownership and understanding.

- Incident Reporting Channels: Establish clear and accessible communication channels for reporting security incidents, ensuring prompt response and investigation.

- Feedback Loop: Create a feedback loop to continuously improve cybersecurity practices, gathering input from employees and adapting strategies based on their experiences.

In the evolving digital landscape, the strength of your organization's defense lies not only in technological solutions but in the collective awareness, actions, and engagement of every team member. By empowering your human firewall with knowledge, skills, and a shared sense of responsibility, you can transform your workforce into a resilient barrier against cyber threats, safeguarding your organization's valuable assets and reputation.

Guarding the Gateways

In the ever-evolving realm of cybersecurity, business leaders face a constant challenge: protecting their organizations from a barrage of sophisticated cyber threats. These threats often infiltrate through common digital "gateways" – email, web browsing, and social media – making it crucial for businesses to fortify their defenses at these critical entry points.

This chapter, "Guarding the Gateways," serves as a comprehensive guide to securing these gateways, empowering business leaders and IT professionals with the knowledge and strategies to safeguard their organizations against cyberattacks. It delves into the specific vulnerabilities and attack vectors associated with each gateway, providing actionable steps and real-world examples to illustrate effective defense measures.

- Securing Email Communications

  Email, a ubiquitous tool for business communication, has also become a prime target for cybercriminals. Phishing attacks, malware distribution, and targeted attacks often originate from seemingly innocuous emails. To combat these threats, businesses must implement robust email security measures:

  - Importance of email security: Understanding the role of email security in preventing phishing attacks, malware distribution, and other email-based threats.

  - Best practices for email encryption and authentication: Implementing email encryption protocols and authentication methods, such as DMARC and SPF, to verify sender legitimacy and ensure secure data transmission.

  - Case studies illustrating the consequences of email-based breaches: Examining real-world examples of organizations that have fallen victim to email-based attacks, highlighting the potential financial, reputational, and operational damage caused by such breaches.

- Web Security Measures and Safe Browsing Practices

  The internet, while a valuable tool for business operations, also harbors a multitude of threats. Malicious websites, drive-by downloads, and other web-based attacks can compromise sensitive data and disrupt business continuity. To navigate the web safely, businesses must employ effective web security measures and safe browsing practices:

- Overview of common web-based threats: Identifying and understanding the various types of web-based threats, including malicious websites, phishing attacks, drive-by downloads, and cross-site scripting (XSS) attacks.

- Strategies for secure web browsing: Implementing strategies for secure web browsing, such as using secure connections (HTTPS), keeping browsers updated, and avoiding suspicious links or websites.

- Real-world examples of organizations falling victim to web-based attacks: Analyzing real-world cases of organizations that have been compromised through web-based attacks, showcasing the impact and consequences of such breaches.

- Managing Cybersecurity Risks in Social Media

Social media platforms, while valuable for brand engagement and customer communication, also present significant cybersecurity risks. Social engineering tactics, fake profiles, and data exposure can lead to unauthorized access, reputational damage, and financial losses. To mitigate these risks, businesses must establish a robust social media cybersecurity policy:

- The growing threat landscape on social media platforms: Understanding the evolving threat landscape on social media platforms, including social engineering scams, fake profiles, data breaches, and manipulation campaigns.

- Risks associated with social engineering, fake profiles, and data exposure: Analyzing the specific risks associated with social engineering tactics, fake profiles, and data exposure, highlighting the potential consequences for businesses.

- Guidelines for creating a robust social media cybersecurity policy: Developing a comprehensive social media cybersecurity policy that outlines acceptable usage guidelines, risk mitigation strategies, and incident response procedures.

- Case Studies of Attacks Through These Vectors

To gain a deeper understanding of how cybercriminals exploit vulnerabilities in email, web, and social media, it is crucial to examine real-world case studies. These case studies provide valuable insights into the methods used by attackers, the impact on targeted organizations, and the lessons learned:

- In-depth analysis of recent cyberattacks that exploited email, web, and social media vulnerabilities: Analyzing recent cyberattacks that have exploited vulnerabilities in email, web, and social media, providing detailed breakdowns of the attack methods, targeted organizations, and the impact caused.

- Examination of the methods used by attackers and the impact on targeted organizations: Examining the specific methods used by attackers in each case study, including the types of malware employed, the social engineering tactics used, and the vulnerabilities exploited.

- Lessons learned from each case study, providing actionable insights for readers: Drawing actionable lessons from each case study, providing readers with practical takeaways to enhance their organization's cybersecurity posture and mitigate similar threats.

- Implementing Robust Defenses Against Each Vector

Armed with the knowledge gained from the preceding sections, businesses can now implement robust defenses against threats that target email, web, and social media:

- Practical strategies for fortifying email security, including advanced threat protection: Implementing advanced threat protection solutions for email, including anti-phishing filters, malware detection tools, and sandboxing capabilities.

- Deployment of web application firewalls and secure Deployment of web application firewalls (WAFs) and secure browsing tools: Implementing web application firewalls (WAFs) to filter malicious traffic and protect against web application attacks, such as SQL injection and cross-site scripting (XSS). Additionally, providing employees with secure browsing tools, such as secure web gateways (SWGs), to prevent access to malicious websites and protect against drive-by downloads.

- Developing a comprehensive social media security strategy, including employee training: Establishing a comprehensive social media security strategy that includes clear guidelines for employee conduct, regular security awareness training, and incident response procedures to address social media-related breaches.

- Proactive measures to detect and respond to threats in real-time: Implementing proactive measures to detect and respond to threats in real-time, such as intrusion detection systems (IDS) and intrusion prevention systems (IPS), to identify and mitigate security incidents as they occur.

By implementing these comprehensive defense measures, businesses can effectively safeguard their email communications, web browsing activities, and social media presence from evolving cyber threats. The insights and strategies provided in this chapter empower business leaders and IT professionals to strengthen their organization's cybersecurity posture and navigate the ever-changing digital landscape with confidence.

The Cyber Resilient Enterprise

In the ever-evolving realm of cybersecurity, staying ahead of the curve is not just an option; it's an imperative. As cyber threats morph and mutate, business leaders face a critical challenge: building organizations that can not only withstand today's attacks but also anticipate and adapt to the challenges of tomorrow. This chapter delves into the concept of cyber resilience, guiding business leaders on how to establish a robust defense system that is not only reactive but also proactive and future-proof.

- Subscribing to Cybersecurity News Feeds

  In today's dynamic threat landscape, staying informed

about the latest cyber threats is crucial. Subscribing to reputable cybersecurity news feeds provides business leaders with real-time insights into emerging threats, attack methods, and vulnerabilities. This continuous stream of intelligence allows them to make informed decisions about their organization's cybersecurity posture and proactively address potential risks.

- Understanding the importance of real-time threat intelligence: Real-time threat intelligence provides organizations with the ability to identify and respond to threats as they emerge, minimizing the potential for damage and disruption.

- Identifying reputable cybersecurity news sources: Subscribing to credible cybersecurity news sources ensures that organizations receive accurate and up-to-date information from trusted experts.

- Establishing a streamlined process for information dissemination within the organization: Effective dissemination of threat intelligence within the organization ensures that all relevant personnel are aware of emerging threats and can take appropriate action to mitigate risks.

- Participating in Cybersecurity Conferences and Training

The cybersecurity landscape is constantly evolving, and staying ahead requires continuous learning and skill development. Participating in cybersecurity conferences and training programs provides business leaders and their teams with access to the latest advancements in cybersecurity knowledge, techniques, and tools.

- The role of conferences in staying updated on industry trends: Cybersecurity conferences serve as a platform for industry experts to share their latest insights, research, and best practices, keeping attendees at the forefront of the ever-changing threat landscape.

- Nurturing a culture of continuous learning among cybersecurity teams: Fostering a culture of continuous learning within cybersecurity teams ensures that they are equipped with the knowledge and skills necessary to address the evolving threats of the digital age.

- Leveraging training programs for skill enhancement and certification: Training programs provide opportunities for cybersecurity professionals to enhance their skills, obtain industry certifications, and stay up-to-date on the latest technologies and methodologies.

- Conducting Regular Security Assessments and Audits

Proactive vulnerability assessments and security audits are essential components of a cyber resilient enterprise. These assessments help identify and address potential security weaknesses before they can be exploited by attackers, minimizing the risk of data breaches and other security incidents.

- The significance of proactive vulnerability assessments: Vulnerability assessments proactively identify weaknesses in an organization's security posture, allowing for timely remediation and prevention of potential breaches.

- Implementing regular security audits to identify weaknesses: Regular security audits provide a comprehensive evaluation of an organization's overall cybersecurity posture, identifying potential risks and areas for improvement.

- Creating a feedback loop for continuous improvement based on assessment results: Establishing a feedback loop ensures that the findings of vulnerability assessments and security audits are used to continuously improve the organization's cybersecurity posture.

- Adapting to Emerging Threats

The cyber threat landscape is constantly evolving, and new threats emerge regularly. To effectively protect their organizations, business leaders must develop a framework for anticipating and mitigating emerging threats.

- Examining historical case studies of evolving cyber threats: Analyzing historical case studies of emerging cyber threats provides valuable insights into how threats evolve, allowing organizations to anticipate and prepare for future attacks.

- Developing a framework for threat anticipation and mitigation: Establishing a framework for threat anticipation and mitigation involves identifying potential threat vectors, assessing their likelihood and impact, and developing plans to mitigate them.

- Cultivating an agile response mechanism to address emerging threats promptly: Maintaining an agile response mechanism enables organizations to quickly adapt and respond to emerging threats, minimizing the disruption and damage caused by attacks.

- Developing a Future-Proof Cybersecurity Strategy

A future-proof cybersecurity strategy is essential for ensuring that an organization's defenses remain effective against the evolving threats of the digital age. This strategy should be aligned with the organization's overall business goals and leverage emerging technologies to enhance cybersecurity capabilities.

- Aligning cybersecurity strategy with overall business goals: Integrating cybersecurity strategy with the overall business strategy ensures that security initiatives are aligned with the organization's objectives and contribute to its success.

- Integrating artificial intelligence and machine learning for predictive analysis: Leveraging artificial intelligence and machine learning in cybersecurity enables organizations to predict potential threats.

Securing Your Tomorrow

As we conclude this journey through the intricate landscape of cybersecurity, we stand at the threshold of a secure tomorrow. Each chapter has served as a beacon, guiding you through the maze of cyber threats and illuminating the path towards a resilient defense.

- Navigating the Digital Peril: Decoding the Ever-Shifting Cyber Landscape

  In an era where digital boundaries blur and threats lurk in the shadows, understanding the ever-evolving cyber landscape is no longer a choice but an imperative. This chapter has equipped you with the knowledge to decipher the motivations behind cyberattacks, empowering you to anticipate and mitigate potential threats.

- Fortifying the Digital Fortress: Laying the Pillars of Cybersecurity

  Cybersecurity is not a fleeting endeavor; it's a continuous process that demands unwavering commitment. By laying the foundations of vulnerability management, access control, data security, and incident response planning, you've constructed a robust digital fortress, capable of withstanding the onslaught of cyber adversaries.

- Empowering the Human Firewall: Educating and Engaging Your Workforce

  Your employees are the first line of defense against cyber threats, yet many lack the awareness and training to identify and mitigate these perils. This chapter has emphasized the crucial role of a cyber-aware workforce, equipping your team with the knowledge and best practices to create an impenetrable human firewall.

- Guarding the Digital Gateways: Securing Email, Web, and Social Media

  Digital gateways serve as entry points for a multitude of cyber threats. By understanding and fortifying email, web, and social media, you've erected formidable defenses against specific attack vectors, ensuring the integrity of these critical channels.
  - Embracing the Ever-Evolving Threat Landscape: Building a Cyber Resilient Enterprise

In the dynamic world of cybersecurity, staying ahead of the curve is not a luxury; it's a mandate. This chapter has guided you on the path to building a cyber-resilient enterprise, emphasizing continuous learning, proactive threat anticipation, and future-proofing your cybersecurity strategies.

- Your Next Steps: Take Action Today!

As we close this comprehensive guide, your journey towards a more secure tomorrow begins. Reflect on the key insights from each chapter, recognizing that cybersecurity is not a one-time event but an ongoing process that demands unwavering commitment. Foster a culture of vigilance within your organization, encouraging continuous learning and adaptation to combat emerging threats.

Call to Action

Implement Cybersecurity Measures Immediately:

- Prioritize the implementation of the strategies outlined in each chapter.

- Ensure that your organization's cybersecurity measures align with the principles of a resilient enterprise.

Stay Informed and Engaged:

- Subscribe to reputable cybersecurity news feeds to stay abreast of emerging threats and trends.

- Actively participate in conferences and training programs to enhance your cybersecurity knowledge and skills.

Conduct Regular Security Assessments:

- Schedule regular vulnerability assessments and security audits to identify and address potential weaknesses.

- Leverage the insights gained from these assessments to continually strengthen your cybersecurity posture.

Adapt and Future-Proof:

- Embrace an agile mindset, adapting your cybersecurity strategies to address evolving threats.

- Develop a future-proof cybersecurity strategy that aligns with your organization's overall business goals.

Remember, cybersecurity is a shared responsibility. Your commitment to securing your organization is not just a shield against threats but a catalyst for future success. For ongoing support, questions, or further engagement, feel free to reach out. Together, we can build a cyber-resilient future where innovation thrives, and digital security prevails. Your journey to securing tomorrow starts now!

With a graduate degree in information security and three decades of hands-on experience in the IT industry, Dr. Kinchen possesses a comprehensive understanding of the ever-evolving cyber threat landscape and the strategies necessary to safeguard your business from cyberattacks. His extensive experience spans a wide spectrum of IT roles, including data management, systems analysis, DevOps, security, cloud operations, data center operations, and architectural design. This diverse background has equipped him with a unique perspective on cybersecurity, allowing him to identify vulnerabilities and implement effective protection measures across all facets of an organization's IT infrastructure.

Throughout his career, Dr. Kinchen has witnessed the rise of sophisticated cyber threats and the devastating impact they can have on businesses. He has been deeply involved in developing and implementing robust cybersecurity strategies for organizations of all sizes, helping them protect their sensitive data, maintain operational continuity, and safeguard their reputation from the damaging effects of cyberattacks.

Dr. Kinchen's expertise extends beyond technical knowledge to encompass a deep understanding of business processes and risk management principles. He is adept at translating complex cybersecurity concepts into actionable strategies that align with an organization's specific needs and objectives. Dr. Kinchen is also passionate about educating and empowering employees to become active participants in cybersecurity, recognizing that human behavior is often the weakest link in the security chain.

As a trusted cybersecurity advisor, Dr. Kinchen is committed to providing businesses with the knowledge, tools, and strategies they need to navigate the ever-changing cybersecurity landscape with confidence. His goal is to help you build a resilient organization that can withstand cyberattacks, protect its valuable assets, and maintain its competitive edge in the digital age.